For C, B♭, E♭ & Bass Clef Instruments

BEBOP ERA

Play-Along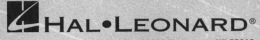

Trumpet: Jamie Breiwick
Alto and Tenor Sax: Eric Schoor
Piano: Mark Davis
Bass: Jeff Hamann
Drums: David Bayles
Recorded by Ric Probst at Tanner-Monagle Studio

To access online content visit:
www.halleonard.com/mylibrary

Enter Code
4752-1903-1168-6521

ISBN 978-1-4950-9472-9

HAL•LEONARD®

7777 W. BLUEMOUND RD. P.O. BOX 13819 MILWAUKEE, WI 53213

For more information on the Real Book series, including community forums, please visit
www.OfficialRealBook.com

Visit Hal Leonard Online at
www.halleonard.com

Contents

Au Privave

(MED. FAST) SWING

— Charlie Parker

C VERSION

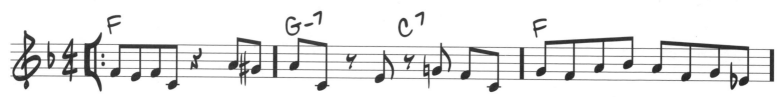

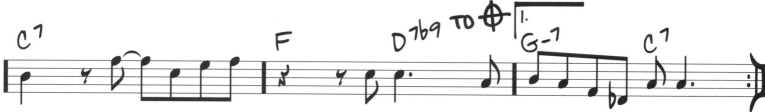

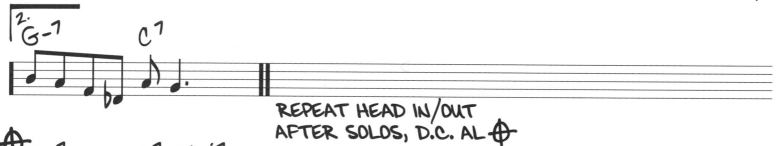

REPEAT HEAD IN/OUT
AFTER SOLOS, D.C. AL ⊕

BONEOLOGY

— J.J. JOHNSON

BOUNCING WITH BUD

- EARL "BUD" POWELL / WALTER GIL FULLER

C VERSION

(MED. UP SWING)

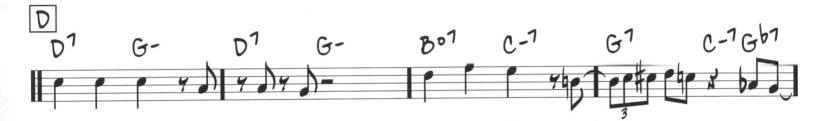

DEXTERITY

— CHARLIE PARKER

(MED. FAST) SWING

C VERSION

*OPTIONAL

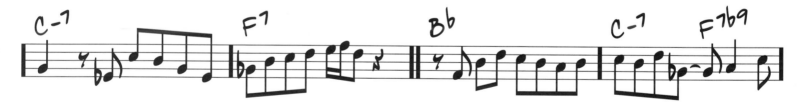

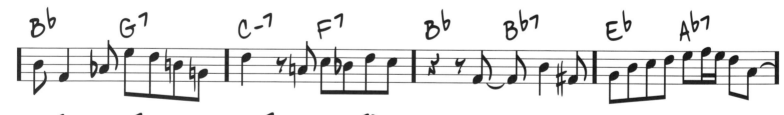

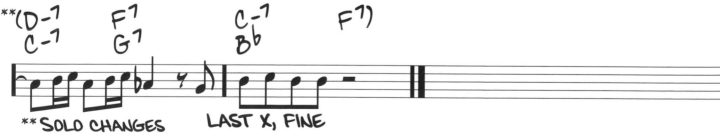

** SOLO CHANGES   LAST X, FINE

GROOVIN' HIGH

(MED. FAST) SWING

— JOHN "DIZZY" GILLESPIE

C VERSION

*(A-7b5)

* SOLO CHANGES

FINE

REPEAT HEAD IN/OUT
AFTER SOLOS, D.C. AL FINE

HALF NELSON

— Miles Davis

(MED. FAST) SWING

C VERSION

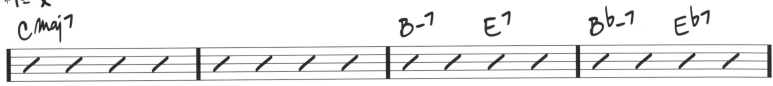

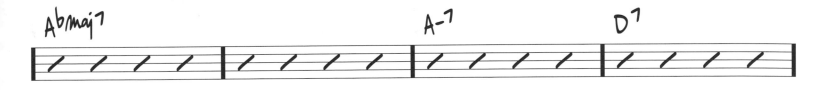

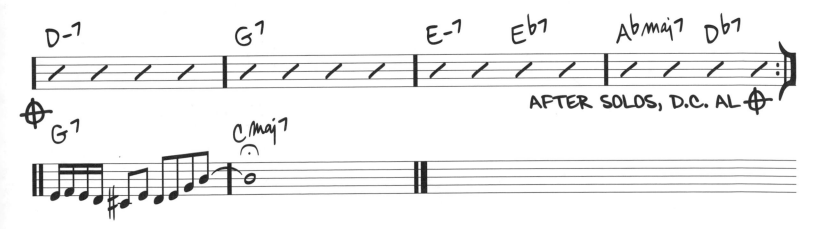

In Walked Bud

— Thelonious Monk

C VERSION

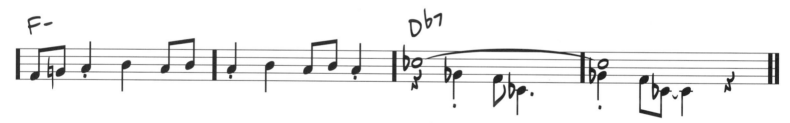
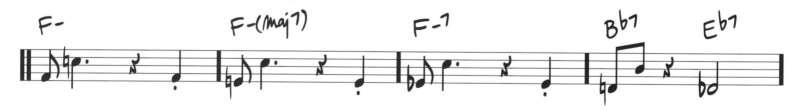

AFTER SOLOS, D.C. AL ⊕
(TAKE REPEAT)

LADY BIRD

– TADD DAMERON

C VERSION

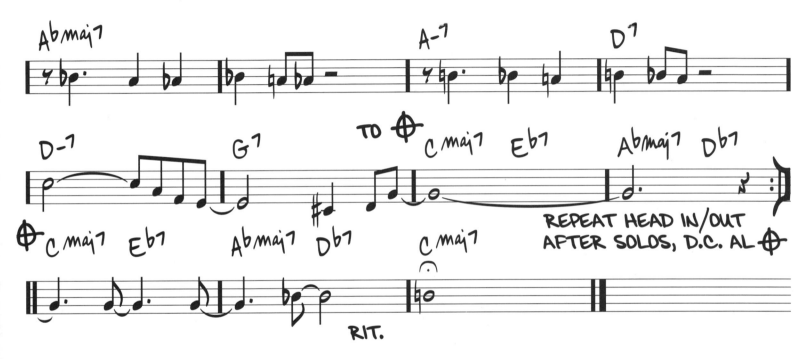

REPEAT HEAD IN/OUT
AFTER SOLOS, D.C. AL ⊕

RIT.

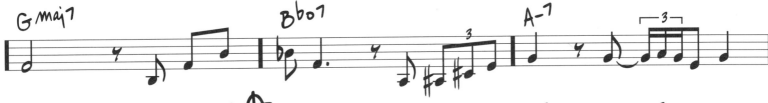

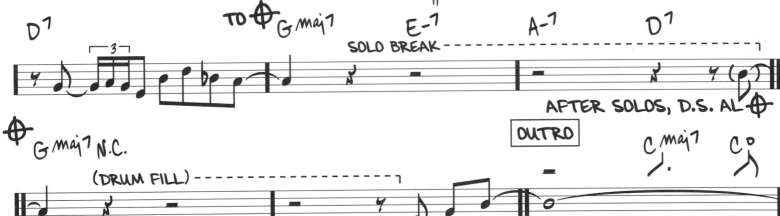

Move

— Denzil De Costa Best

C Version

(up)

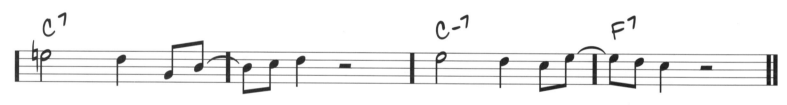

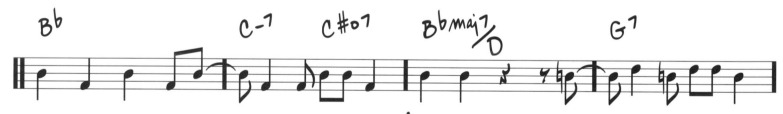

FINE

Au Privave

- Charlie Parker

(MED. FAST) SWING

B♭ VERSION

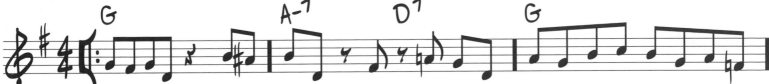

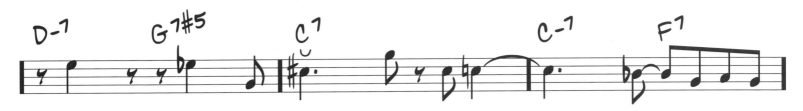

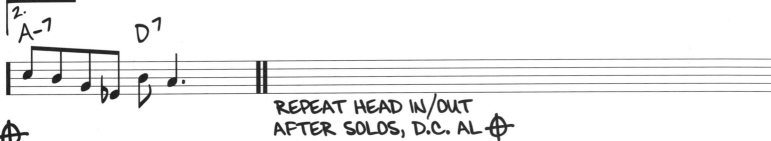

REPEAT HEAD IN/OUT
AFTER SOLOS, D.C. AL ⊕

Boneology

— J.J. Johnson

DEXTERITY

— CHARLIE PARKER

Bouncing With Bud

- Earl "Bud" Powell/Walter Gil Fuller

Bb Version

(MED. UP SWING)

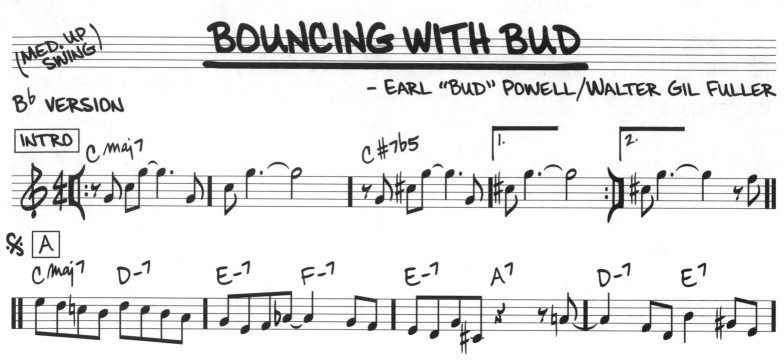

Groovin' High

— John "Dizzy" Gillespie

(MED. FAST)
SWING

B♭ Version

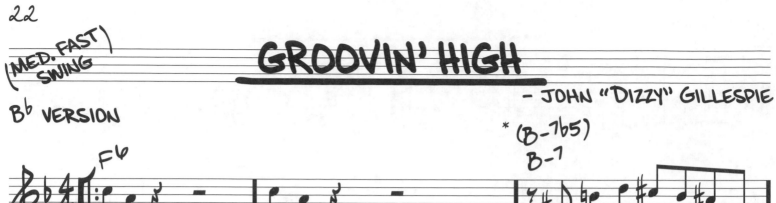

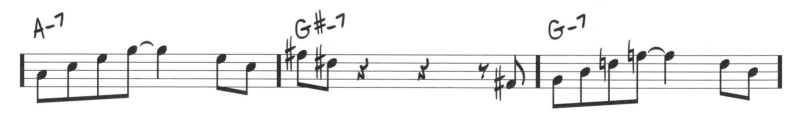

FINE   REPEAT HEAD IN/OUT
AFTER SOLOS, D.C. AL FINE

IN WALKED BUD

— THELONIOUS MONK

(MED. FAST) SWING

Bb VERSION

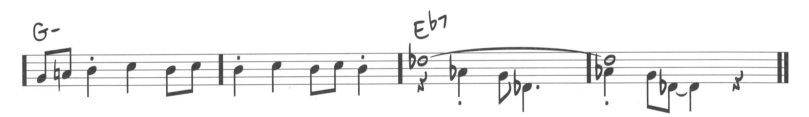

AFTER SOLOS, D.C. AL ⨁
(TAKE REPEAT)

HALF NELSON

— Miles Davis

(MED. FAST) SWING

Bb Version

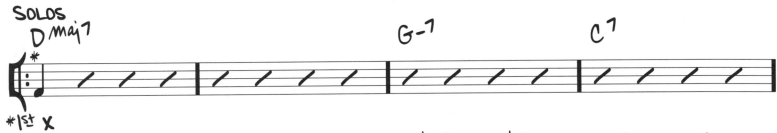

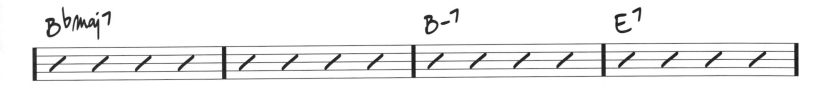

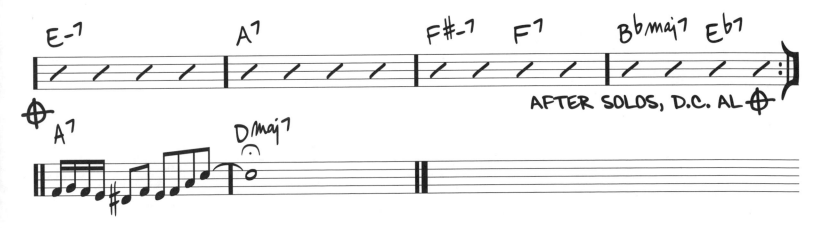

Lady Bird

— TADD DAMERON

REPEAT HEAD IN/OUT
AFTER SOLOS, D.C. AL ⊕

RIT.

Move

— Denzil De Costa Best

B♭ Version

Witches Pit

— Pepper Adams

Au Privave

— Charlie Parker

(MED. FAST) SWING

Eb VERSION

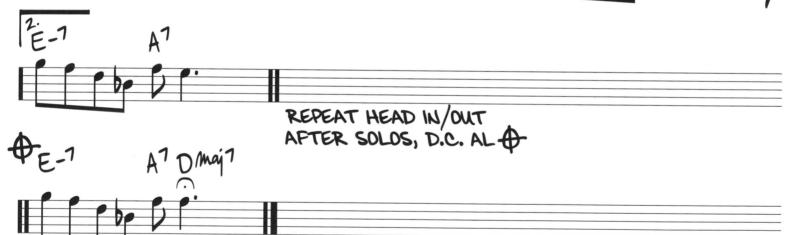

REPEAT HEAD IN/OUT
AFTER SOLOS, D.C. AL ✛

BONEOLOGY

— J.J. JOHNSON

Eb Version

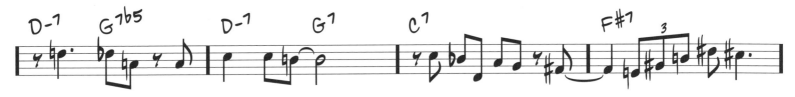

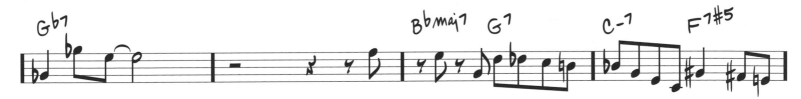

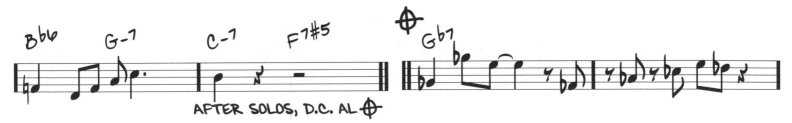

AFTER SOLOS, D.C. AL ⊕

Bouncing With Bud

— Earl "Bud" Powell/Walter Gil Fuller

Eb Version

(MED. UP SWING)

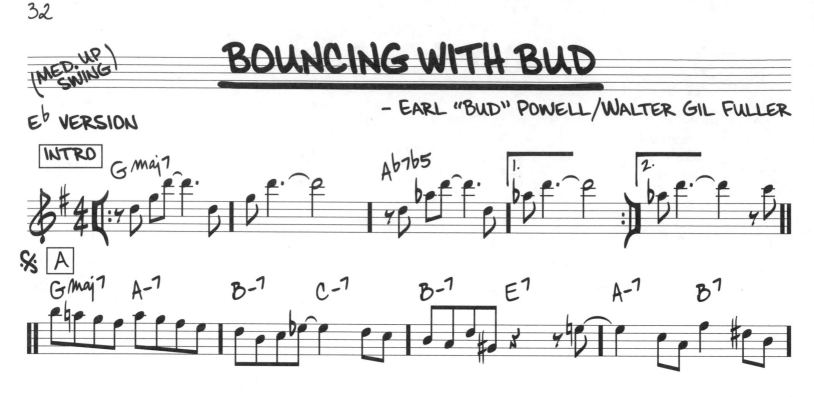

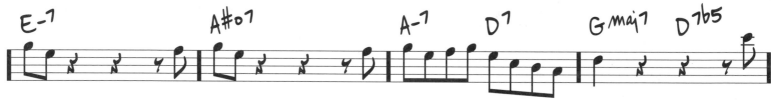

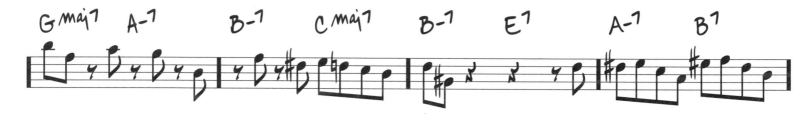

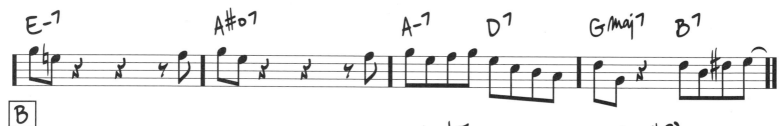

*SOLO CHANGES

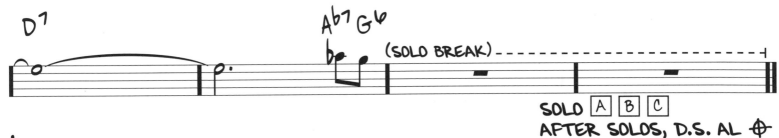

SOLO A B C
AFTER SOLOS, D.S. AL ⊕

DEXTERITY

Groovin' High

— John "Dizzy" Gillespie

Eb VERSION

(MED. FAST) SWING

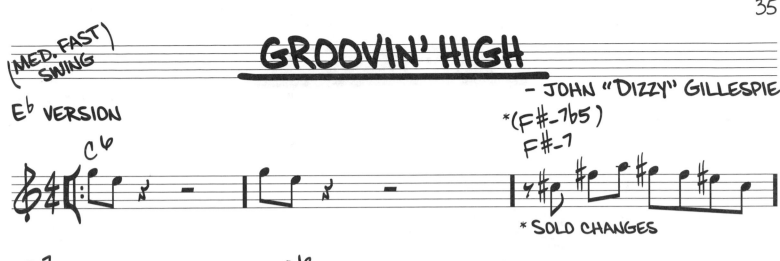

*(F#-7b5)
F#-7

* SOLO CHANGES

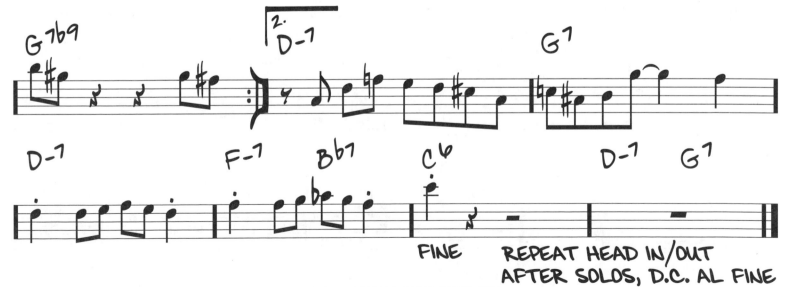

FINE

REPEAT HEAD IN/OUT
AFTER SOLOS, D.C. AL FINE

HALF NELSON

— Miles Davis

(MED. FAST) SWING

E♭ Version

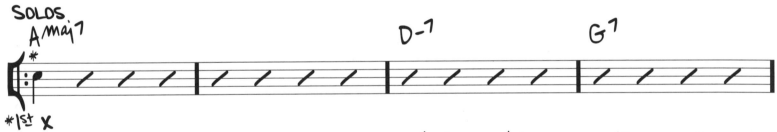

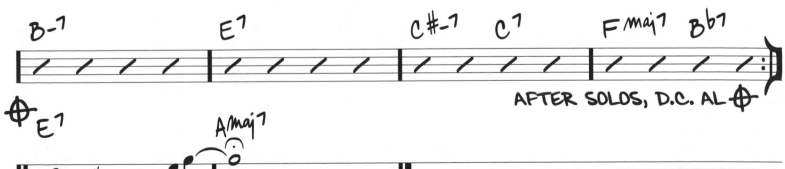

AFTER SOLOS, D.C. AL ⊕

In Walked Bud

— Thelonious Monk

(MED. FAST) SWING

Eb Version

AFTER SOLOS, D.C. AL ⊕
(TAKE REPEAT)

Lady Bird

— TADD DAMERON

REPEAT HEAD IN/OUT
AFTER SOLOS, D.C. AL

RIT.

Witches Pit

— Pepper Adams

Eb Version

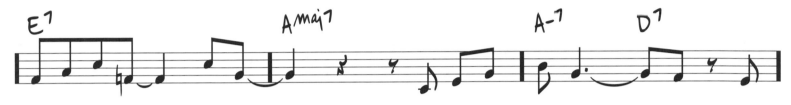

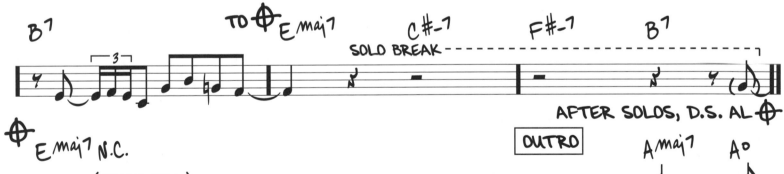

MOVE

— Denzil De Costa Best

(UP)

Eb VERSION

TO ⊕

AFTER SOLOS, D.C. AL ⊕
(TAKE REPEAT)

FINE

Au Privave

- Charlie Parker

9: C VERSION

REPEAT HEAD IN/OUT
AFTER SOLOS, D.C. AL ⊕

BONEOLOGY

- J.J. JOHNSON

DEXTERITY

(MED. FAST) SWING

𝄢: C VERSION

– CHARLIE PARKER

** SOLO CHANGES   LAST X, FINE

BOUNCING WITH BUD

— EARL "BUD" POWELL/WALTER GIL FULLER

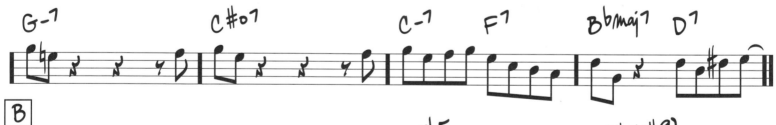

Groovin' High

— John "Dizzy" Gillespie

(MED. FAST) SWING

C Version

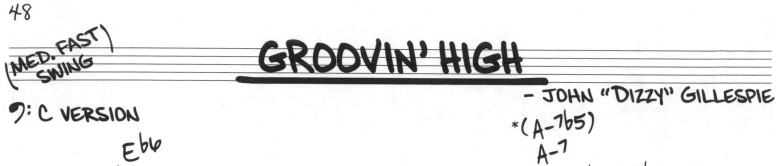

*(A-7b5)
A-7

* SOLO CHANGES

FINE

REPEAT HEAD IN/OUT
AFTER SOLOS, D.C. AL FINE

In Walked Bud

— Thelonious Monk

(MED. FAST) SWING

C VERSION

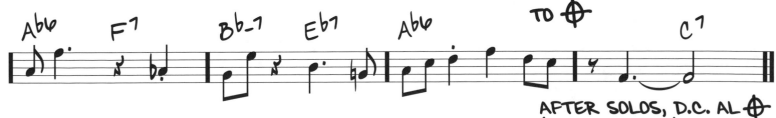

AFTER SOLOS, D.C. AL ⊕
(TAKE REPEAT)

HALF NELSON

— MILES DAVIS

9: C VERSION

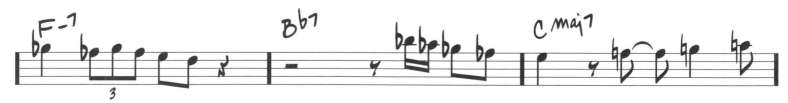

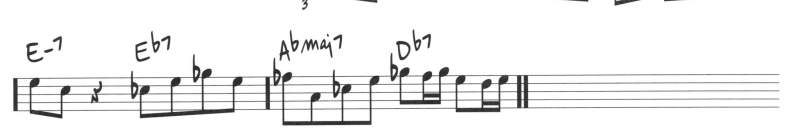

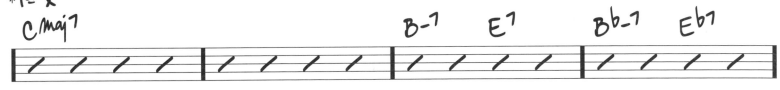

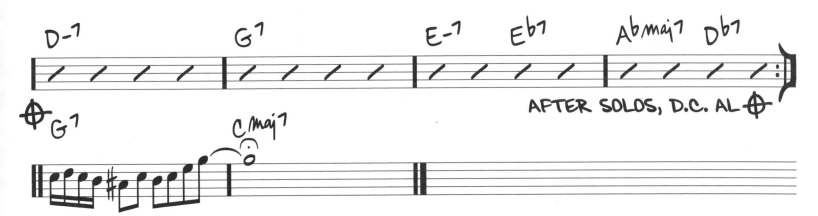

Lady Bird

— TADD DAMERON

REPEAT HEAD IN/OUT AFTER SOLOS, D.C. AL ⊕

RIT.

Move

- Denzil De Costa Best

Witches Pit

— Pepper Adams

THE REAL BOOK MULTI-TRACKS

TODAY'S BEST WAY TO PRACTICE JAZZ!
Accurate, easy-to-read lead sheets and professional, customizable audio tracks accessed online for 10 songs.

1. MAIDEN VOYAGE PLAY-ALONG
Autumn Leaves • Blue Bossa • Doxy • Footprints • Maiden Voyage • Now's the Time • On Green Dolphin Street • Satin Doll • Summertime • Tune Up.
00196616 Book with Online Media...$17.99

2. MILES DAVIS PLAY-ALONG
Blue in Green • Boplicity (Be Bop Lives) • Four • Freddie Freeloader • Milestones • Nardis • Seven Steps to Heaven • So What • Solar • Walkin'.
00196798 Book with Online Media...$17.99

3. ALL BLUES PLAY-ALONG
All Blues • Back at the Chicken Shack • Billie's Bounce (Bill's Bounce) • Birk's Works • Blues by Five • C-Jam Blues • Mr. P.C. • One for Daddy-O • Reunion Blues • Turnaround.
00196692 Book with Online Media...$17.99

4. CHARLIE PARKER PLAY-ALONG
Anthropology • Blues for Alice • Confirmation • Donna Lee • K.C. Blues • Moose the Mooche • My Little Suede Shoes • Ornithology • Scrapple from the Apple • Yardbird Suite.
00196799 Book with Online Media...$17.99

5. JAZZ FUNK PLAY-ALONG
Alligator Bogaloo • The Chicken • Cissy Strut • Cold Duck Time • Comin' Home Baby • Mercy, Mercy, Mercy • Put It Where You Want It • Sidewinder • Tom Cat • Watermelon Man.
00196728 Book with Online Media...$17.99

9. CHRISTMAS CLASSICS
Blue Christmas • Christmas Time Is Here • Frosty the Snow Man • Have Yourself a Merry Little Christmas • I'll Be Home for Christmas • My Favorite Things • Santa Claus Is Comin' to Town • Silver Bells • White Christmas • Winter Wonderland.
00236808 Book with Online Media...$17.99

10. CHRISTMAS SONGS
Away in a Manger • The First Noel • Go, Tell It on the Mountain • Hark! the Herald Angels Sing • Jingle Bells • Joy to the World • O Come, All Ye Faithful • O Holy Night • Up on the Housetop • We Wish You a Merry Christmas.
00236809 Book with Online Media...$17.99

The interactive, online audio interface includes:
- tempo control
- looping
- buttons to turn each instrument on or off
- lead sheet with follow-along marker
- melody performed by a saxophone or trumpet on the "head in" and "head out."

The full stereo tracks can also be downloaded and played off-line. Separate lead sheets are included for C, B-flat, E-flat and Bass Clef instruments.

HAL•LEONARD®
www.halleonard.com

Prices, content and availability subject to change without notice.